D0206200

More Praise for *Opening Doors to Teamwork and Collaboration*

"From the deeply personal to the cosmically universal, we each know the value of opening doors to others. We may sometimes forget how to do that, so thanks, Judith and Fred, for the gift you have placed in our hands."

—Doug O'Loughlin, **Principal Consultant, Civil Service College Centre for Organisation Development, Singapore**

"Fred and Judith have created a practical guide for achieving breakthrough change through a simple approach to mastering interactions. I know it works because I have had the benefit of using the four keys on a daily basis over the last four years to drive quicker and better business decisions and outcomes in two different organizations. This book is a must-read for those who want all team members to be and feel like they are a key part of the solution."

—Stan Howell, **Plant Manager, Pennsylvania**

"Companies of all sizes can benefit from the notions, stakes, boulders, and tombstones terminology. Using notions and stakes creates a much more collaborative environment because they invite conversation. Likewise, organizational waste is reduced with the use of boulders and tombstones because people clearly understand the intensity of the opinion. Four simple words make a *big* impact."

—Kathy Clements, **Vice President for Culture and Inclusion, Ecolab**

"Judith and Fred continue their marvelous way of engaging us and reminding us of how to collaborate effectively. As two experienced and encouraging guides, they walk us through an open door from behaviors that impede collaboration to behaviors that can change the quality of our relationships and enhance our work with others."

—John D. Vogelsang, **Editor-in-Chief, *OD Practitioner***

"'Share your Street Corner' builds upon the accumulated wisdom of many years in the trenches. Both timely and timeless, its core precepts and principles are key to successful employee creativity, engagement, and inclusion."

—Thomas Kochman, **COO, Kochman Mavrelis Associates, Inc., author of *Black and White Styles in Conflict*, and coauthor (with Jean Mavrelis) of *Corporate Tribalism***

"*Opening Doors* is the natural follow-up to *Be BIG* and *The Inclusion Breakthrough*. Katz and Miller further hone their ideas regarding enhanced pathways for high-performance institutions by providing 'four keys' to success."
—Bailey W. Jackson, EdD, **Emeritus Professor of Social Justice Education, University of Massachusetts Amherst**

"The *Opening Doors* journey starts with the concept of 'joining' the team...all in, as an ally, accepting that no one is perfect, assuming positive intent, and bringing the teaming skills described in the book to the workplace. It can change careers and lives."
—Steve Fritze, **retired CFO, Ecolab**

"These keys are crucial for melding disparate individuals into high-performing teams. While the authors do not mention the word *diversity*, I predict that *Opening Doors* will be a significant addition to diversity literature."
—R. Roosevelt Thomas, Jr., **CEO, Roosevelt Thomas Consulting and Training**

"Loaded with nuggets of wisdom, this book effectively captures intrapersonal, interpersonal, organizational, and societal implications and proactive actions for 'changing everything' for the better for all involved."
—Michael L. Wheeler, **Associate Director, Diversity, Omnicom Media Group, and former Program Director and Research Associate, The Conference Board**

"Never underestimate the power of simplicity! *Opening Doors* is a case in point. This small but formidable book has BIG concepts that are as easy to implement as one, two, three, four."
—Cindy Szadokierski, **Vice President International Airport Operations, The Americas, Atlantic and Pacific, United Airlines**

"Companies expanding globally, or even into a new market segment, will benefit from Fred and Judith's advice to share their street corners. We've learned that we make better decisions when we seriously consider the full spectrum of viewpoints, especially when the street corners range from St. Paul to St. Petersburg. By encouraging leaders to stay curious and seek a wide range of perspectives, this book helps organizations increase their potential for breakthrough thinking."
—Douglas M. Baker, Jr., **Chairman and CEO, Ecolab**

"This is an excellent read with practical solutions to workplace challenges, such as stating one's intent and intensity, interspersed with short examples to help the busy executive avoid misunderstandings, waste, and missteps. These ideas are simple yet powerful ways to enhance clarity of purpose, communication, and productivity in a more positive, collaborative work environment!"

—Eunice Chan, **Managing Consultant, Caliper Human Strategies, Singapore**

"*Opening Doors* gives you the keys to unlock the potential of any organization by getting communication right the first time. Fred and Judith have done it again, and that is a tombstone."

—Hal Yoh, **Chairman and CEO, Day & Zimmermann**

"Collaboration is an essential ingredient to build a successful workplace. Judith and Fred's work has been meaningful in the development of our organization. This book provides practical tools to help build these important skills. We can't do it alone—working better together is vital for our future."

—Eileen Fisher, **founder and Chief Creative Officer, Eileen Fisher, Inc.**

"*Opening Doors* is special: it describes key resonating principles to guide leaders in organizations so they can quickly unleash the potential and contribution of their people."

—David Wilks, **Wilks & Partners, UK**

"By hearing different perspectives, we are able to create innovative ways of doing what we need to do. But we don't often hear how to create this space. This book gives concise, practical how-to steps to bring about the inclusive workplace we desire."

—Steve Humerickhouse, **Director, Multicultural Forum on Workplace Diversity**

"I especially loved 'Share Your Street Corner.' And next time I facilitate a community meeting, you can bet I will be asking myself, 'Are all the right people in the room?'"

—Denise Cerreta, **founder, One World Everybody Eats Foundation**

"An elegantly simple framework for building effective partnerships and teams. This little book distills a great deal of experience into a few key principles."

—L. David Brown, **Senior Research Fellow, Hauser Center for Nonprofit Organizations, Harvard University**

"This book opens the doors for all organizations to change the world of work. Just the chapter on 'Listening as an Ally' can do more to help organizations create a positive sense of unity, productivity, and shared direction than spending millions of dollars on more complicated approaches."

—Darya Funches, EdD, **former Chair of the Board, Organization Development Network and National Training Laboratories Institute for Applied Behavioral Science, and founder and Principal, REAP Unlimited**

"I have experienced that when I am passionate during a discussion, my passion can easily be misinterpreted as a requirement or order. With the simple construct of 'notions, stakes, boulders, and tombstones,' conversations become unambiguous; everyone knows what's being requested and what is open for discussion (or what can be ignored completely!). No more guessing, 'What did he mean by that?' or 'Was that a request or just a thought?' That allows me to be passionate without worrying about what people may think I said: a win for everyone involved!"

—Michael Thien, **Senior Vice President, Global Science, Technology, and Commercialization, Fortune 100 Company**

"*Opening Doors* is an enjoyable and accessible read that offers helpful tips, insightful examples, and important advice for bringing out the best in ourselves and our colleagues. I look forward to bringing the lessons to my organization."

—Liz Maw, **CEO, Net Impact**

"Few organizations today can give time to members to develop the comfort level to build trust so they can work together to bring about organizational change. Fred and Judith bring to focus the awkwardness individuals experience when practicing new behaviors that are desired for organizational transformation."

—Yeo Keng Choo, **Managing Director, Caliper, Singapore**

"I wish I had heard of the concept of listening as an ally thirty years ago. It really captures the attitude that has been in the room during the major collaborative breakthroughs of my career. I know this will help my team develop the trust to make those breakthroughs happen much more frequently."

—Jim Miller, **Executive Vice President and President, Critical Global Initiatives, Ecolab**

"Much has been written about 'getting it right' in the modern manufacturing environment (Lean, Six Sigma, TQM, etc). The focus is usually on removing waste from business processes or from human-machine interactions. *Opening Doors* shows how to remove waste from human-human interactions, arguably the most abundant type of waste and until now the most ignored."
—Hugh McDonald, **Plant Product Manager, UK**

"Judith and Fred are brilliant change agents! These skills allow all of us to be more effective cross-cultural communicators and to engage in truly productive and motivating discussions. The exercises in understanding the degrees of someone's intent, the repercussions of how projects are communicated, and real-life scenarios will permanently remove the guesswork from your conversations."
—Cassandra D. Caldwell, PhD, **founder and CEO, International Society of Diversity and Inclusion Professionals**

"I particularly identified with the section on 'leaning into discomfort,' as I have long been an admirer of what Abraham Lincoln was able to accomplish with his 'team of rivals.' Katz and Miller provide clear, easy steps to strong leadership skills. Skills that lead to a style of leadership, which empowers everyone and maximizes organizational success."
—Susan C. Scrimshaw, PhD, **president, The Sage Colleges, Troy, NY, USA**

"For those who lead institutions of higher education, learning how to encourage faculty and staff to respectfully 'share your street corner' is particularly relevant in the rapidly evolving higher education landscape."
—Christine B. McCormick, PhD, **dean, School of Education, University of Massachusetts, Amherst**

"A valuable and practical guide to developing the muscles necessary to build a high performance organization through 4 practices. Think of it as 'circuit training' for organizations. The wisdom of this book is that the real key to leadership is doing what is difficult, modeling it, and facilitating it for team members. They call it 'leaning into discomfort.' They correctly identify it as being fundamental to the other three practices."
—Farha-Joyce Haboucha, **director, Sustainability and Impact investments, Rockefeller & Co. (The views expressed are hers alone.)**

Opening Doors

to Teamwork and Collaboration

Opening Doors

to Teamwork and Collaboration

4 Keys That Change EVERYTHING

Judith H. Katz & Frederick A. Miller

FOREWORD BY WILLIE DEESE

Berrett–Koehler Publishers, Inc.
San Francisco
a BK Business book

Illustrations by Jeevan Sivasubramaniam

Berrett-Koehler Publishers, Inc.
235 Montgomery Street, Suite 650
San Francisco, CA 94104-2916
Tel: (415) 288-0260
Fax: (415) 362-2512
www.bkconnection.com

Ordering Information

Quantity sales. Special discounts are available on quantity purchases by corporations, associations, and others. For details, contact the "Special Sales Department" at the Berrett-Koehler address above.

Individual sales. Berrett-Koehler publications are available through most bookstores. They can also be ordered directly from Berrett-Koehler: Tel: (800) 929-2929; Fax: (802) 864-7626; www.bkconnection.com.

Orders for college textbook/course adoption use. Please contact Berrett-Koehler: Tel: (800) 929-2929; Fax: (802) 864-7626.

Orders by U.S. trade bookstores and wholesalers. Please contact Ingram Publisher Services: Tel: (800) 509-4887; Fax: (800) 838-1149; E-mail: customer.service@ingrampublisherservices.com; or visit www.ingrampublisherservices.com/Ordering for details about electronic ordering.

Berrett-Koehler and the BK logo are registered trademarks of Berrett-Koehler Publishers, Inc.

Printed in the United States of America

Berrett-Koehler books are printed on long-lasting acid-free paper. When it is available, we choose paper that has been manufactured by environmentally responsible processes. These may include using trees grown in sustainable forests, incorporating recycled paper, minimizing chlorine in bleaching, or recycling the energy produced at the paper mill.

Library of Congress Cataloging-in-Publication Data
   Katz, Judy H., 1950–
     Opening doors to teamwork and collaboration : 4 keys that change everything / Judith H. Katz, Frederick A. Miller ; foreword by Willie Deese. — First edition.
     pages cm.
   ISBN 978-1-60994-798-9 (pbk.)
    1. Teams in the workplace. 2. Interpersonal relations. 3. Organizational effectiveness. 4. Organizational behavior. I. Miller, Frederick A., 1946– II. Title.
   HD66.K377 2013
   658.4'022—dc23   2013000832

First Edition

17 16 15 14 13 | 10 9 8 7 6 5 4 3 2 1

Produced by BookMatters, cover designed by Brian Murray, copyedited by Tanya Grove, proofed by Anne Smith.

With love to David Levine, my husband. You hold the key to my heart and steadfastly open the door to my staying honest with myself and loving life every day. Your integrity, insights, and values are key to our living a meaningful life. To Fred Miller, thank you for bringing your brilliance and creativity to our partnership. Your *Street Corner* always opens up new doorways and breakthroughs in our working together. It has been 28 years and going strong! And to the people in KJCG and our clients, thank you for trusting in me, for challenging me, and for helping me to continue to grow and learn with you. You open the door to new ways of being on this journey of life, and for that I am eternally grateful.

—JHK

Our third book. I always thought I would write a book, and thank you, Judith H. Katz, for making that dream come true three times and counting. You are a gift in my life and the best business partner in the world. Of course, I have to appreciate my 100+1-year-old mother. Every day in my life she has been an inspiration to me. Thank you, Mom, for giving me so many, many gifts. Thanks to Pauline for her love and our 30 years of marriage; and thanks to Kamen and Shay, our two wonderful children, for all the lessons you have taught me—I love you. And, finally, the wonderful people in The Kaleel Jamison Consulting Group—every day you open doors for me.

—FAM

A special dedication to Edith Whitfield Seashore (1928–2013) guide, mentor, sage, and dear friend. Thanks for your many, many gifts. You will be greatly missed.

—FAM & JHK

Contents

Foreword

by Willie A. Deese, President,
Merck Manufacturing Division

I was extremely pleased when Fred and Judith asked me to write the foreword to *Opening Doors to Teamwork and Collaboration: 4 Keys That Change Everything.* For more than three decades, we exchanged ideas and worked together to improve organizational environments from the computer industry to the pharmaceutical industry. What I learned through our collaboration has expanded my view and understanding of transformational cultural change in ways that I could not have imagined 30 years ago.

My mental model of a high-performing organization began 35 years ago while working for the Digital Equipment Corporation in Massachusetts. It was a workplace where everyone had the opportunity to do their best. I share this from the perspective of a country boy from North Carolina born in the '50s and raised at a time when not everyone was afforded equal opportunities.

Since then, I've had the privilege to lead national, international, and global organizations that ranged in size from 500 to 30,000 employees, with some spanning more than 30 countries. Through these experiences, I've come to some conclusions that are fundamental to the way I motivate people and lead organizations.

It's clear to me that people genuinely want to meaningfully contribute and achieve their highest possible potential. They want to work in a place where they are listened to, heard, valued, and respected. And, most of all, they appreciate and enjoy hearing the words "thank you" for a job well done. By realizing this, we are all given the opportunity to improve performance outcomes in organizations everywhere, regardless of our industry, cultural norms, regional practices, language, country, city, neighborhood, or "street corner."

So why isn't more being done to inspire high-performing organizations today? Because it's not easy; in fact, it's darn difficult! It requires leaders to change behaviors and build capabilities to lead and manage in a different way. But the benefits are worth making the changes, changes which this book will clearly explain.

I've worked in companies that placed high value on technical knowledge and skills. These attributes are typically required of high-performing individuals, but are they enough? Do they alone create an environment that allows everyone in the organization to truly do their best work and achieve their full potential? Do these attributes alone help sustain high performance and enable organizational success? I don't think so. I believe teamwork, collaboration, and trust are the missing pieces needed to complete the high-performing organization puzzle.

I invite you to unlock the high-performing potential of your organization through the *4 Keys That Change Everything*. They can help leaders, like you, deliver transformational organizational change.

Lean into discomfort. Be willing to have difficult, straight-talk discussions about performance and expectations up, down, and across the organization. It gets easier with each discussion. In my experience, when these conversations take place with care and concern, people know you want them to succeed.

Listen as an ally. Demonstrate respect for your team members and allow for the exchange of thoughts and ideas that lead to better outcomes.

State your intent and intensity. Leave little room for misunderstanding, but allow others to discern appropriately whether your decisions and expectations can be influenced. In other words, stakes are firmly positioned but movable. Boulders are heavy but can be moved with effort. Tombstones aren't movable.

Share your street corner. Be open and willing to listen to others' views from *their* "street corners" to broaden your understanding across the organization.

Applying these 4 Keys—Lean into Discomfort, Listen as an Ally, State Your Intent and Intensity, and Share Your Street Corner—will unlock the high-performing potential of your organization. In my experience, when the 4 Keys are embraced by people committed to leading in this way, they root teamwork, increase collaboration, and enhance organizational trust, which in turn deliver faster, stronger, and more sustainable business results.

By exploring and embodying the 4 Keys, you can achieve the results I've seen throughout my career in organization after organization. It may be difficult at first, but as Andrew Carnegie said, "Anything in life worth having is worth working for."

Leading and managing in this way will inspire your team to do their best, and that changes *everything*!

Welcome to Opening Doors

CHANGE THE INTERACTION.
CHANGE THE EXPERIENCE.
CHANGE THE RESULT.

The basic building blocks of organizations are our interactions. This book offers a simple method for improving those interactions.

The work and the working environments of organizations are the sum of countless daily interactions. They are the very fabric and foundation of teamwork and collaboration.

While technology is enabling faster and better connectivity, human connection is moving at a much slower pace. In this time of so much change and so many unknowns and unknowables, our human interactions are not keeping pace.

Having clear interaction is critical, and yet we seem to find less time and less capability to understand each other. We expect *Right First Time* technological solutions, but we rarely expect or experience *Right First Time* human interactions. And while we may have tools to provide greater technological connectivity, we often lack the tools for human interaction connectivity.

Organizations are only as productive as the interactions that take place among individuals, teams, and work groups. Very few organizations address the quality of interactions, and—no surprise—very few organizations have been able to create the sense of excitement, energy, productivity, and shared mission that occurs when people truly join each other and experience strong, positive, collaborative, and productive interactions.

Opening Doors offers ways to have better, more productive, more satisfying interactions—*Right First Time* interactions—because increasingly, that first time may be only one of a few opportunities we get.

The Keys That Open Doors to Better Interactions, Teamwork, and Collaboration

Can you remember your early days on a new job? You felt excited, maybe a little scared. You saw doors opening for you to bring your skills to your team.

But over time, you became aware of how some doors closed when you felt judged by others. You stopped sharing a difference of opinion for fear of being seen as an outsider, and you did not feel safe to speak up. Other doors closed when you did not feel heard or took unneeded actions because you misinterpreted what people wanted or meant.

How often do the doors to greater teamwork and collaboration close—or never open—because people . . .

- don't trust each other?

- don't feel safe to speak up?

- misunderstand each other's intent?

- don't want to hear different points of view?

How much energy is wasted trying to figure out what is the right key that will unlock the door?

The power of the 4 Keys is that they work! They provide a common language to behaviors that is easily understood and that everyone can use. They open the doors to teamwork and interaction. And when the doors open, inside are the rewards of greater trust, collaboration, understanding, and breakthroughs.

Since we wrote *Be BIG: Step Up, Step Out, Be Bold* in 2008, we have seen the impact the book has made on people's lives at all levels of organizations. People who once felt small found ways to be BIG—BIGGER than they could have imagined. People easily use the language of *Be BIG*; this alone helps them have the courage to raise issues and to challenge team members in a joining way to accomplish more together than they could alone. *Be BIG* continues to make an impact on how individuals see themselves, see their colleagues, and engage together as team members to achieve so much more. Just the notion of Being BIG and stepping up has changed lives.

The journey toward higher performance and the ability for individuals and teams to work more effectively together begins with Being BIG. That is an important start—to have the courage and to see the possibility of being better individually and collectively. But all too often, people struggle with *how* to Be BIG—how to unleash their own and their team's potential. What is needed to help people Be BIG is to unlock the doors to improving human interactions, and the 4 Keys That Change *Everything* do just that.

That is the power of the 4 Keys—it is not magical; it is not complicated. It just takes a willingness to apply these behaviors to change your interactions.

This book is for anyone from the shop floor to the executive suite in search of higher performance, greater collaboration, faster and better decision making, stronger problem solving, and the ability to create breakthroughs. For individuals and teams in organizations around the globe, these 4 Keys have opened doors to improved performance. So . . .

- *if* you want to experience greater trust, understanding, collaboration . . .

- *if* you need to generate greater productivity and transformative breakthroughs . . .

- *if* you are ready to achieve more with others than you can alone . . .

. . . then read on, and doors will open for you and your team members too.

A NOTE ABOUT THE VOICES IN THE 4 KEYS

In addition to the "we" voice—the voice of the authors, Judith and Fred—there are several other voices used in the book.

A voice explores the concepts of the book:

Appearing as first-person experience and is printed in blue type like this.

And as illustrated characters when providing their insights:

This voice appears in typeface like this.

There is also an "I" voice that questions and has doubts:

"This voice appears in quotes like this."

If this multiple-voice approach feels unfamiliar, we hope you will *Lean into Discomfort* and hang in there with us. We hope you will *Listen as an Ally* to try to understand the Keys from the perspectives of individuals who have actually worked with them. We hope the different voices help to clarify the *Intent and Intensity* of these Keys—what they are, how they are experienced by people in organizations, and how they work in real-life situations. And by *Sharing* our *Street Corner* with you, we hope it becomes clear that this process of listening to and joining with multiple voices—the reality of teamwork and collaboration—is the surest route to the breakthroughs we are all looking for in our organizations, our work, and our lives.

Introduction

4 KEYS THAT CHANGE EVERYTHING

We know this is a BIG statement. These 4 Keys *do* change *every* interaction. We have seen it. We have lived it. And yes, we understand why you might be skeptical.

We would doubt such a BIG claim. But we have observed these keys at work in organizations all over the world.

The Keys provide a common language that everyone can use. They are simple and powerful.

KEY #1 LEAN INTO DISCOMFORT
Opening the Door to Trust

KEY #2 LISTEN AS AN ALLY
Opening the Door to Collaboration

KEY #3 STATE YOUR INTENT AND INTENSITY
Opening the Door to Understanding

KEY #4 SHARE YOUR STREET CORNER
Opening the Door to Breakthroughs

KEY #1 OPENS THE DOOR TO TRUST

Opening this door feels like I am taking a risk, but if I want greater teamwork and collaboration, I need to Lean into the Discomfort I feel in order to get to know you better. How else can we work together? How else can we solve problems and eliminate confusion and wasted effort?

When I Lean into Discomfort I help make it safer to be honest and open with you. As I feel safer and you feel safer, we can open the Door to Trust. Unless I am willing to Lean into Discomfort, the door to those possibilities and potential will remain closed.

KEY #2 OPENS THE DOOR TO COLLABORATION

When I Listen as an Ally, it enables me to hear what you, my team members and colleagues, are saying, and all of us to build on each other's ideas.

Slowing down to hear you is the key that unlocks the door to collaboration, which results in faster achievement of our goals.

KEY #3 OPENS THE DOOR TO UNDERSTANDING

When you State Your Intent and Intensity, it helps me, my team members, and my colleagues take the guesswork out of suggestions or directions and opens the door to greater understanding of each other. Stating my Intent and Intensity does the same for you.

As the door to understanding is opened, I see how to contribute more quickly, confidently, and decisively. When I know how best to contribute, I know how to add value; and if you do the same, we can each add greater value. And this combined greater value results in our saving time as we achieve Right First Time interactions.

KEY #4 OPENS THE DOOR TO BREAKTHROUGHS

When you Share Your Street Corner and I share mine, we learn to hear differences as contributions, rather than as sources of conflict. As we share our different perspectives, we can see the fuller 360-degree view, use our combined resources, and achieve breakthroughs none of us could have envisioned or accomplished alone.

By using all 4 Keys, the doors to trust, collaboration, and understanding are opened, and the door to breakthroughs unlocks.

Using the 4 Keys Starts with Joining

Judging or Joining? Every interaction begins with this critical decision, and it impacts everything that follows. We do it so quickly and automatically that we are usually not even aware of it.

When I meet you, do I join you—see you as a friend, an ally, someone on the same side of the table? Or do I judge you—size you up, wonder if you are someone not to be trusted, engage cautiously with you, and deny you the benefit of the doubt?

If I decide to join you, I treat you as someone worthy of respect. I listen, am open, extend trust, share information. I am willing to have honest and perhaps difficult conversations. I seek to learn from you. I give you the benefit of the doubt.

If I truly want to open doors to teamwork and collaboration, I need to start by seeing what I could gain from joining you.

Rather than believing I am better off going it alone, I begin to believe that the best way to succeed is through partnership and collaboration. And by joining you, I am investing in our partnership with the expectation that we will connect and together do great things.

If we begin by truly joining, we have the ability to open many doors and unlock the potential and power each of us can bring to the team and to the larger organization. But we have heard others say . . .

66Joining is difficult.99

66It is hard to trust others and to earn their trust.99

66It is hard to listen to others, especially when they are not saying things I want or expect to hear.99

66It is hard to define my intentions clearly when others aren't defining theirs.99

66And it is very, very hard to actively seek out and support perspectives that are different from my own to make sure all Street Corners are heard from.99

We used to think these things too.

But when we began to observe the 4 Keys in action, we noticed that people quickly made them a way of life in their organizations—and in their personal lives as well. People actually like to practice these simple Keys; and when used, these 4 Keys change *Everything*. We invite you to join us as we open new doors.

Opening the Door to

Key #1: Lean into Discomfort

Lean into Discomfort

- TAKE RISKS: experiment with new behaviors and actions.

- SPEAK UP: address issues.

Everything new feels uncomfortable at first, which is why discomfort is a prerequisite for learning, growth, and change.

For most people, trusting others—and truly joining them—is challenging, and that can be uncomfortable.

Discomfort does not always mean stop and run for cover.

Some things that make me uncomfortable are just unsafe situations and not great ideas to pursue. The discomfort I may feel when someone suggests bungee jumping into a volcano, for example, is a useful warning to heed.

But what about when I feel discomfort interacting with new team members because I am unsure of what they bring to the team or what working with them will be like? Avoiding those interactions is not the best course of action.

The same goes for the discomfort I might feel when I need to work with someone in another department or whose language is different, or when I need to present new ideas in front of a room of leaders.

If I discover the sky is falling, then yes, I should probably run. But most of the time, discomfort is just a signal that I need to pay attention to something new and different. That includes opportunities to make a contribution. And on some occasions, it is a signal not just that something is different, but that I have an opportunity to make a difference.

Discomfort is a signal that alerts us to possible opportunities for learning, growth, and change.

Discomfort means:
PAY ATTENTION!

Watch out for
Change, Opportunity,
Learning, Growth

What does *discomfort* have to do with *trust?*

When we talk to people in organizations about how to *Lean into Discomfort* as the key to opening the *Door to Trust*, we often hear the following:

> "I am comfortable with the people I trust, and I only trust people with whom I am comfortable."

Trusting others—especially people outside our closest circle of family, friends, colleagues, or team members—is often uncomfortable. And most of the time we avoid discomfort as a matter of course.

But today's organizations don't have the time to wait for people to develop the comfort levels usually required to build trust, so *Lean into Discomfort* needs to be an unwritten part of our job descriptions.

Trust is fundamental for our most productive interactions. Without trust, our interactions are flawed at best, destructive at worst, and uncomfortable always. When you *Lean into Discomfort,* you make it possible to open the door to an environment in which trust can grow quickly.

We avoid situations that make us feel uncomfortable. If THIS way feels uncomfortable, we tend to go THAT way.

When we open the door and *trust* . . .

- we are willing to give each other the benefit of the doubt.

- we expect to connect and gain something from our interaction.

- we listen more attentively and appreciatively to one another.

- we look for the value in what our colleagues say and build on that.

- we show we are willing to act in spite of our discomfort, trusting our partners to have our backs.

- we let our partners know we have *their* backs and that they can trust us.

- team members are more likely to extend trust to us.

- we support and encourage our team members to Be BIG, step out, and *Lean into Discomfort* as well.

- we are more willing to join together, share information, and get to root causes of difficult issues more quickly.

- we know we will get better as we work together and learn from one another.

- we are more likely to act like a team.

- we collaborate more effectively.

- we are open and willing to be innovative.

When you consider the alternative, if you could choose trust, why wouldn't you?

Change Requires Us to *Lean into Discomfort*

Change can be hard. But in today's global marketplace, the ability to learn and adapt to a constantly changing environment is a critical skill—for each of us as individuals and for our organizations as well. To respond to the hastening pace of technological and social change, we need to be able to step outside our comfort zones and change the way we work individually and collectively, in established work groups, across departments, as part of ad hoc teams, and virtually across the globe. Few of us can afford *not* to change.

Given a choice between feeling comfortable and feeling uncomfortable, I will choose comfort most of the time. But should I make that choice?

Staying in our comfort zones may feel familiar, safe, and secure, but it is very hard to be open to anything new.

I can't keep doing things the same old way and expect the results to ever be any different.

There's another reason each of us often resists change:

> 66 If something I have been comfortable doing has been working well enough to produce success, it doesn't make sense to change it. That is just common sense: don't mess with success. 99

But increasingly, that bit of common sense is making it harder for individuals to adapt to changing conditions. And conditions keep changing rapidly, both in our organizations and in the world. When what worked yesterday stops working today, we probably need to try something new.

So what's stopping us from wanting to *Lean into Discomfort*?

> 66 I tried to raise an issue once. I learned my lesson. It is not safe to be open and honest here. 99

> 66 I'm busy right now. I'll get around to it when things slow down. 99

> 66 It feels awkward. I don't want to make a fool of myself. 99

- When *is* the right time to *Lean into Discomfort*? *The answer:* usually as soon as we notice there *are* issues and begin to feel a sense of discomfort that something is not quite right. That is the time to say: "I am going to be courageous, Be BIG, and *Lean into Discomfort* to address this issue now."

- Often when something feels risky we find ways to put it off, hoping the issue will just go away. But if *now* is not the right time, when *is*? If we put it off, aren't we just trading one set of problems for another? If addressing the issue this way will create greater trust, eliminate waste, or prevent bigger problems down the road, isn't this *exactly* the right time to *lean in*?

- Many new and different behaviors start out feeling awkward and abnormal. So we need to practice leaning in so it will become less and less awkward. And pretty soon, leaning in will become the new normal.

When we Lean into Discomfort, it enables greater collaboration as we trust each other to say the things that need to be honestly said without fear of being judged or second-guessed.

The cost of *not* creating trust

I may be reluctant to Lean into Discomfort and trust others because I have been hurt before. Or because I fear others will take advantage of me. Or because I believe they must earn my trust.

But the cost of not trusting is high. Without trust, we . . .

- waste our time and energy in judging and feeling judged.

- are more guarded toward each other.

- don't easily build on each other's ideas.

- have more difficulty supporting each other's growth.

- speak only when we are certain.

- close the door to opportunities for more productivity and efficiency, and also for more creativity and joy.

Creating
safety is not
a passive act.

So how do we make it safer to *Lean* in?

If we only did what was safe, we would never have learned to ride a bicycle. Sure, we might have skinned our knees and fallen a few times, but that didn't mean we stopped trying. As toddlers, if we had stopped trying to stand and walk because of how often we fell, we would still be crawling. Just about every new skill is awkward and possibly embarrassing in the beginning—but that should not stop us from learning and growing.

To help create safety (for ourselves and others), we need to . . .

- Share with others what we need to feel safe.

- *Lean into Discomfort* and speak up when we don't feel safe.

- ask others what they need to feel safe so they can *Lean* in with us.

- reach out to extend safety to others—even if they differ from us.

- be brave and at times be willing to be *first*.

Creating safety does not mean eliminating risk

Creating the safety needed to *Lean* in does not mean creating a risk-averse environment, or even a risk-free environment. It means fostering an environment that respects and acknowledges the differing approaches and experiences of all team members, and what each of us needs to feel safe so we can do our best work. It means putting as much (or more) effort into psychological and emotional safety as some organizations do for physical safety.

The goal is an environment in which we each feel psychologically and emotionally safe enough to trust that others *have* our back rather than *stabbing* us in the back—an environment in which we can speak up without fear of retribution, an environment where we trust each other. An environment where we *all* can succeed.

One way I encourage others to Lean into Discomfort: I go first!

When we *Lean into Discomfort*, we . . .

- are more willing to share our ideas.

- are more willing to try new techniques and learn new skills.

- are more likely to lend a hand to the person in the next cubicle.

- are more welcoming to colleagues we meet in the elevator or walk by in the hallways.

- are more likely to say hello to colleagues who look familiar but whose names we don't know.

- don't take crazy or unwarranted risks, but are willing to take worthwhile risks.

- are willing to talk about the elephant in the room—even if others are not willing to address it or admit that it is there.

- know that if things don't work out, at least we did our part.

The cost of creating an emotionally unsafe environment is high. So much goes unspoken, and so much talent is left behind . . .

Delayed Gratification

After noticing how new team members were often excluded from informal planning sessions and lunch meetings, Mike decided to *Lean into Discomfort* by raising the issue in the next staff meeting. He prefaced his remarks with "I'm going to *Lean into Discomfort* to raise an issue that is keeping us from using all our resources as well as we could."

The room was quiet after he spoke. The team leader responded by saying, "We always try to make the best use of everyone's skills. Does anyone have a response to Mike's remarks?"

But no one said a word, and the leader went on to the next item on the agenda. Mike was worried that he had wasted his breath and damaged his standing with the team leader and the team.

After all the agenda items had been discussed, the team leader returned to the issue Mike raised. "Earlier in our meeting, Mike suggested that, as a team, we are not doing a good job of using all the resources of our team. And when I asked whether anyone had a response to Mike's observation, I heard no responses."

The leader looked around the conference table. The room was full of uncomfortable people.

"I learned three things from Mike's comments, and from the team's lack of response" said the leader. "First, I learned that as a leader, I am not doing a good enough job of encouraging and requiring all of us to bring our voices into meetings and planning sessions. Second, I learned that our newer staff members are not feeling safe enough or invited enough to fully contribute. And third, I learned that the rest of you are not feeling safe enough or supportive enough to respond to comments like Mike's, whether you agree or disagree."

The leader was quiet. Slowly, the team members began to speak up, sharing their ideas about what was blocking them from speaking up and ways to better utilize team members' experiences.

The resulting surge in energy and engagement started with one person *Leaning into Discomfort*, and it changed everything for Mike and the team.

Do YOU feel safe enough to STEP OUT?

And the *Door to Trust* Starts to Open . . .

That's why the first Key to changing *Everything* is to *Lean into Discomfort*.

"I am going to *Lean into Discomfort* and . . ."

One of the best ways to model how to Lean into Discomfort is by letting others know when I am doing it.

By establishing a common language and using those actual words, I signal to others that I am reaching out and extending trust, willing to be vulnerable, and extending an invitation to reciprocate.

When I Lean into Discomfort, *I encourage others to reach beyond their comfort zones and join me in creating a more engaging and productive workplace environment.*

When I say, "I am going to Lean into Discomfort," *it is an invitation for others to* Listen as Allies *and to find ways to join me. (See chapter 2, coming up in just a few pages!)*

It is a simple equation: as I lean in, others become more willing to lean in. As we all lean in together, greater trust is created, greater synergies are created, and greater teamwork and collaboration become possible.

New Route to Success

As we were beginning work with his company, a hardworking senior leader described some of the ways he tried to be efficient with his time. One way was by taking a shortcut from the parking garage to his desk. It enabled him to avoid the delays and distractions of having unscheduled conversations with people along the way. As an introvert, this also allowed him to avoid having to talk and interact with lots of people on the way to his office, which to him seemed like a good idea.

As we discussed the importance of workplace interactions, he realized that he had lost connection with the people in his organization. He decided to *Lean into Discomfort* by taking a new route that would bring him into contact with his team members rather than avoid them.

The first week or so, the route took a long time as he said hello to people and began to ask them questions about their work and their lives. Some had a lot to say, including things that were uncomfortable for him to hear. Some people had stored up a lot of issues they wanted to discuss with him if they ever got the opportunity, and believing this might be their *only* opportunity, they told him all that they had stored up.

But after those first few weeks, as his practice of walking the halls in the morning continued, the exchanges became faster and friendlier. People learned to trust that he would be back and that he would follow up on issues they raised. He learned a great deal about issues that impacted his ability to lead and manage the organization, and he was able to assist others in their ability to get things done more quickly as well.

The new route started with *Leaning into Discomfort,* but it became the leader's New Normal.

Oh, Yes I Do!

In a high-volume manufacturing plant, a work team was meeting to address some critical quality and productivity processes. One of the team members, Martha, said to the team and the leader, "I need to *Lean into Discomfort* right now . . ." and proceeded to raise some challenging issues that the team members knew about but had been avoiding speaking about directly.

The team leader's response was, "You don't need to say that! It is safe to raise any issue here."

But Martha replied, "Oh, yes I do. I need to say 'I am going to *Lean into Discomfort'* because those words help me be brave."

Martha went on to describe the issue, and the team had a very productive discussion about some of the things that were blocking their effectiveness and ability to deliver on time. After the meeting, the team leader thanked Martha for leaning in, and thanked the team for the great conversation.

Martha's willingness to *Lean into Discomfort* was the key to greater productivity for the team.

It took one person to *Lean* to open that door.

When I LEAN in, I make it safer for others to LEAN in TOO. Which, in turn, opens the door to greater teamwork and collaboration.

Checklist for Leaning into Discomfort

- ☑ Use the language "I am going to *Lean into Discomfort*" to signal you are moving out of your comfort zone and inviting others to join you.

- ☑ *Lean in* by taking small steps—sitting up front when you normally sit in the back, speaking up when you ordinarily would be silent.

- ☑ Discuss what you need in order to feel safe to speak up.

- ☑ Invite others to discuss what they need to feel safe to speak up.

- ☑ Acknowledge and support other team members when they *Lean into Discomfort.*

Opening the Door to

... COLLABORATION

Key #2: Listen as an Ally

Listen as an Ally

- ## LISTEN AS A PARTNER:
  be ready to join the other person—and give the person the benefit of the doubt.

- ## LISTEN FULLY:
  respond with nonverbal communication as well as words, and check in with the speaker to confirm you understand what is being said.

- ## GIVE ENERGY BACK:
  engage in a spirit of building on what was said.

Allies are willing to work a little harder to hear, understand, appreciate, and build on others' ideas. Are you willing to Listen as an Ally?

Are we all in this together?

"Are we all in this together?" should not be the first question that comes to my mind as I start my workday because it shouldn't be a question at all. The knowledge that we are all in this together to achieve common goals should be the basis for all my interactions, decisions, and actions throughout my day at work, every day. It should be the foundation—the given.

But in too many organizations, people have a very narrow sense of "we." Often it is more like *us* versus *them*. And when we ask if we are all in *this* together, people have different ideas about what *this* refers to. Instead of a shared sense of purpose and joint effort, there are conflicting priorities and competition for information, attention, and advantage. And even *together* doesn't feel like reality. Too often, these words sound less like a genuine question and more like pie-in-the-sky sentiment that prompts eye-rolling and gets ignored, especially when it is not tied to a reward system or how people really work in the organization. People and organizations may *say* they are *all in this together*, or even aspire to be so, but it definitely isn't how they act.

So before we can open the door to collaboration—before we can even *want* to open the door to collaboration—each of us needs to answer that simple question: *are we all in this together?*

Collaboration at times has been used to describe something traitors did with the enemy. And in many organizations, it is still treated that way. In too many organizations, too many people . . .

- criticize colleagues to promote their own positions.

- hoard information to reinforce power and keep ahead of others.

- keep their ideas to themselves to avoid criticism.

- define their immediate work team as part of their "we," but rarely extend that "we" to include people outside that team or in another division or department.

 When I look at you as outside of my "we," I am quick to judge you, reluctant to join you, and rarely give you the benefit of the doubt. I keep the door to collaboration closed.

Without a sense of "we," it is *impossible* to achieve . . .

- shared purpose.

- shared effort.

- shared excitement.

- shared success.

Creating a "We": A Community of Effort

When United Airlines was reinventing itself out of bankruptcy, its former CEO Glenn Tilton said, "We have to create a Community of Effort to succeed."

A Community of Effort is an extended sense of "we"—the sense that yes, we *are* all in this together. And getting there requires one to *Lean into Discomfort* and move beyond the boundaries of the self and the cubicle.

It means moving from a *judging* mindset to a *joining* mindset with our work colleagues.

It means . . .

- seeing them as our partners.

- seeing them as friends and allies.

- seeing them as people who are on the same side of the table, not the opposite side.

It means expanding the boundaries of our comfort zones and extending trust to welcome the fresh perspectives and energies of new team members. It means seeing different perspectives as opportunities and energy toward solving problems, not as oppositional.

It means building cooperative, collaborative, mutual working relationships by linking our ideas together to create something better than any of us could have done individually.

Yes, but before I can expect to build a community with worthy allies, I have to know what it means to be a "we," to be a partner, to be an ally—and be willing to be one.

And before I can experience the sense that we are all in this together, I need to want to be part of something bigger than myself and to help create a new sense of "we."

But often is it difficult to create a "we" and to *Listen as an Ally . . .*

I get the memo announcing the time and agenda for today's staff meeting and I groan. I can't help myself. Most of my colleagues feel the same way about our staff meetings. We talk about them as "boring," "painful," and a "waste of time."

When I get to the meeting, Clarice starts talking about her project, and I start tuning out. She is not in my work group, so I have little interest in her report. I wasn't asked to contribute, so why should I pay attention? Her area is different from my area of expertise, so I am not sure that she would be interested in what I might have to contribute anyway. And besides, I have my own report to give, and I am mentally rehearsing my presentation while trying to assess my manager's mood today.

Meanwhile, sitting next to me, another colleague, Ajay, is excitedly squirming in his seat. He doesn't have a report on the agenda today, but he has good news about a development that is likely to please our leader, and he is looking for an opportunity to speak. He is not really listening to Clarice either. He is waiting for her to finish or to pause for breath so he can jump in and share the news.

As Clarice continues her presentation, others around the table interrupt her with questions about possible shortcomings and flaws:

"Did you run this through legal?"

"Did you consider how our affiliates might react?"

"Have you researched what our competition is doing about this?"

"On slide 20, I think you could have said that a better way."

"I think you are wrong about your eighth point."

As I watch Clarice's confidence erode, I realize my report is scheduled next. Uh oh! After the comments Clarice got, I am not looking forward to being the next person on the chopping block.

But when people see themselves as a "we" and Listen as Allies . . .

I smile when I get the memo about the meeting. I am looking forward to getting together because the meetings are lively and engaging. Everyone leans into the conversations and wants to contribute. When we are together, real progress is achieved, good things usually happen as people build on each other's ideas, and the outcome is greater than any one individual's contribution.

When Clarice starts talking about her project, I listen attentively and with interest. Her work group is accomplishing important things for the organization, and I think of ways I can support them as well as how that work might impact me and my team's work.

My responses and questions and those from others around the table focus on clarifying and improving our understanding of her team's work and finding the connections to what our teams are doing to ensure alignment across our different groups. And while my work

group's professional discipline is different from hers, I think my different perspective might be useful.

When Clarice finishes her report, I mention that something my work group has been working on might help her work group make their process more effective. She asks for details. Others around the table offer examples and suggestions from their own areas that make the collaboration sound especially promising. Before moving on to the next agenda item, team members express their appreciations for what she and her team shared and what they each learned as a result of the conversation.

As Clarice sits down, I can see that she feels her contribution made a difference to the group. She felt *heard* and came away with some promising new avenues to pursue in continuing the project.

And now that it is my turn to present, I feel energized and eager to share my report with the team with the anticipation that new doors will open through our conversation.

Just another ordinary staff meeting. But what a difference!

I assume that if something is important or of interest to you, it will be of interest to me.

Like a Friend

The concept of *Listening as an Ally* came out of a workshop we were giving for leaders of a change initiative in a large multinational organization.

We were discussing the importance of listening and the differences in the ways we listen to our friends versus people we do not see as friends. With friends, we are ready from the outset of an interaction to join with them, assume positive intent, work a little harder to understand their points of view, support them, second their ideas, and build on their ideas.

When we pointed out how rare it is for people in organizations to listen to others as supportively as they do to their friends, one of the participants said, "Well, this may require me to *Lean into Discomfort* just a little, but from now on, I am going to listen to *everyone* as a friend!"

If you succeed,
it is good for me too!

To *Listen as an Ally* means . . .

- listening to find value rather than to find flaws.

- assuming good intent, even if there are flaws or missteps.

- taking the time to put in the effort to hear and understand fully what is being shared.

- checking in with the speakers to find out if our understanding is correct—to let them know what we heard and to let them know that they *have* been heard.

- listening from a learning posture instead of getting ready to respond or interrupt.

- starting with an assumption that we can connect and work to find the places of connection.

- listening with the intent to join, offering appreciation, and contributing to the interaction.

Listening as an Ally Enables the Discovery of Common Interests

We each play roles in our team's and our organization's success, so things that affect either of us should be of interest to both of us.

When I start with the assumption that I want to interact with my team members or other teams as allies—that we want to open the door between us and join our efforts—then each of us will be more willing to reveal what we are thinking, and we all benefit.

Listening as an Ally Enables Us to Find Our Common Good

Often people *say* they are working for the common good and shared success, but in reality they have conflicting objectives or see the priorities in a different order. This often leads to beneath-the-surface conflicts that are rarely identified or addressed and can get in the way of higher performance.

When we each *Listen as an Ally*, we work together to get underneath our assumptions, identify and work through our conflicts, and construct an aligned image of what shared success looks like.

Listening as an Ally Enables Us to Link Our Ideas, Thoughts, and Feelings

I can foster collaboration by linking to another's ideas and acknowledging other's contributions.

When I build on someone else's idea rather than rejecting and offering an alternative to it, it shows I recognize value in that idea. It encourages others to combine energies to achieve collective success instead of competing against each other to achieve individual success at the expense of the team.

And it can be as simple as substituting the words "Yes, and . . ." for the words "Yes, but . . ."

When I link to someone's thoughts and feelings as I Listen as an Ally, it lets that person know, "Yes, you have been heard."

Yes, and . . .

Listening as an Ally Enables Us to Give Energy Back

When I acknowledge someone's hard work, courage, or innovative idea, it encourages a repeat performance and a greater investment of energy and effort the next time. Verbally appreciating others' contributions gives energy back by providing feedback and letting them know how they made a difference to me. This helps build our connection. It encourages the sense of a Community of Effort in which all of us recognize and support each other's contributions.

Giving energy back to you makes you feel more valued and engaged. We can give energy back by . . .

- calling out the parts of what was shared that we would underscore.

- being specific about the parts we found most helpful, and why.

- sharing what we learned and the insights we took away.

- giving thanks for the person's thinking, time, energy, and contributions to moving things forward.

Giving energy back enhances
our interactions, reinforces
partnership, and builds
a community of allies.

Listening as an Ally Is Not about Sugarcoating or Avoiding the Truth

When I Listen as an Ally, I need to be honest and convey authentic, useful feedback. I show my respect for you by giving you my true perspective, which I assume you will appreciate more than some sugarcoated response.

And when I am in meetings or gatherings of colleagues where Listening as an Ally has not been the normal way of interacting, I may not find it safe or comfortable at first. It may require me to Lean into Discomfort.

But think about it like this: when you are talking to someone, would you like that person to *Listen as an Ally*? If so, it's time for you to Listen as an Ally to others.

Seeking clarification and shared understanding will improve the communication in the room for everyone.

When you *Listen as an Ally* to one person, there is a benefit to all.

Listening as an Ally Also Means to Challenge as an Ally

When we *Challenge as an Ally,* we provide new ways of thinking and seeing what was presented in the spirit of an ally, not a judge. We offer alternative perspectives, approaches, and solutions without the claim that they are more valid than the original thought—only that it might add some value from another perspective or *Street Corner.*

When we each *Challenge as an Ally,* we are *partnering*—seeing ourselves on the same side of the table—and seeking ways to help enhance what has been said or done, not to detract from or diminish it.

When we fail to *Challenge as an Ally*—whether by not expressing options for enhancement, attacking what is being shared, or avoiding engagement—we pay a price: we all end up with less.

If each of us doesn't *Challenge as an Ally* . . .

- I may leave thinking that everything I presented was fine, but my team members may feel that what I shared was missing the mark. However, I will not know that and will therefore not perform as well as I could.

- I might think that I just wasted my time and that my team members don't care or are not invested in my or our team's success because we failed to engage.

- I may feel attacked, diminished, or threatened (instead of supported and challenged) and will be less likely to make the effort to present my fullest or most creative ideas in the future.

And if I am not challenged at all, learning opportunities are lost.

Overcoming the "No, No, No!" Reaction

Sitting in a product development meeting, a leader, Sarah, listens as one of her team members makes a suggestion for a new product that is way out of line with the types of products they have been developing. Internally, her first response is, "No, no, no! There is no way that will work."

Instead, Sarah decides to *Listen as an Ally*—she encourages the team member to say more. As other team members listen, they get excited. Sarah invites them to share their opinions about the possible new product and how they could make that work. Team members build on each other's ideas and explore where the ideas take them.

After much conversation, the group concludes that the original suggestion is not workable, but as a result of their conversation the team identifies several new options.

If Sarah had gone with her initial "no" response, the idea would have been shot down and the team's thinking would not have evolved. Because Sarah was able to *Listen as an Ally* and engage with curiosity and encouragement, she enabled an outcome that otherwise would not have been imagined.

So what's stopping us from wanting to *Listen as an Ally?*

> "We have to maintain our standards. How can we maintain quality if we can't ask the hard questions?"

> "Nobody around here acts that way. We are all grown-ups here. We don't need to listen in any special way."

> "I really don't have time to listen. If I give you an opening, you may go on and on all day."

- Sometimes we are so focused on thinking about what we want to do or say that it is difficult to slow down enough to listen fully to what someone else has to say. To *Listen as an Ally* takes patience, and we are often in a hurry. But there is a huge cost when we have to rework and revisit discussions because we haven't fully listened and engaged. If each of us doesn't take the time to *Listen as an Ally*, we can miss important information that will impact our ability to achieve our goals in a timely manner. Sometimes it's best to slow down in order to speed up.

- Some people worry that if they *Listen as an Ally*, they won't be able to express disagreement or say things that are difficult to say. When we *Listen as an Ally*, we start by looking for the value in what others have to offer, but we would not be good allies if we ignored the flaws and errors and ways to improve on what was offered. To *Listen as an Ally* does not mean one lowers standards or avoids conflicts. To *Listen as an Ally*, one must *Challenge as an Ally*, but it must be done with respect and in the spirit of true joining.

- If we want a higher-performing team and greater collaboration, maybe it's time to listen to our colleagues, one of the most important things we can do. Fundamentally, every person wants to feel listened to. That is one of the most important things we can do for our team members.

Present to Us Again, Sam

His last presentation to the Senior Leadership Group several months ago had been so upsetting that Sam vowed he would not do another one. At that meeting the leaders sat with their laptops open and either attacked the presentation or paid more attention to their emails than to Sam. Since that time, many of his best ideas were never shared. But Sam had heard that things had changed. Leaders were focusing on modeling new behaviors and had made a commitment to *Listen as an Ally* and to *give energy back*.

Sam, however, did need to give another presentation. Upon walking into the room, Sam noted a difference in the leaders' behaviors. He was greeted by name and people shook his hand. Laptops were closed and phones out of reach. As he shared his presentation, people actively listened and appreciated his work and his ideas. When he was done, people linked to his ideas and talked about what they learned from his presentation and appreciated about it. They offered improvement suggestions about areas for further exploration and enhancement. Although they had questions and comments about the project, they discussed it as allies, building on Sam's ideas rather than attacking them.

Sam left the meeting energized to continue his work on this project, feeling he had the backing and support of the leadership team.

Checklist for Listening as an Ally

- ☑ Let others know you need them to *Listen as an Ally* as a way to signal that you need their full attention.

- ☑ Give your full attention to others when they are speaking. Don't multitask.

- ☑ Make eye contact and ensure your body language is giving the message "I am joining with you as a partner."

- ☑ Restate what you have heard to check that you are receiving the intended message. Use clarifying questions and language that seeks to understand, such as "Let me check that I understand" and "What I heard you saying was . . . "

- ☑ Accept that what others are saying is true for them and that their perspectives (their *Street Corners*) may be different from yours but no less valid.

☑ After having listened actively, deeply, fully—and making sure you understand their meaning from their point of view—engage with the speakers by respectfully and honestly sharing what you heard as an ally.

☑ Express your appreciation for what was shared. Give energy back!

opening the Door to...

Key #3:
State Your
Intent and
Intensity

State Your Intent and Intensity

Share whether your statement is a

- NOTION: an initial idea

- STAKE: an idea you're committed to, but can be moved

- BOULDER: an item requiring action, with little room for negotiation

- TOMBSTONE: a nonnegotiable position (Act or else!)

In other words,
I say what I mean
and how much I mean it.

This seems so elementary

When I say what I mean, it eliminates guesswork. When I make people guess my Intent, there is a strong possibility they will guess wrong—which guarantees that effort, resources, and time will be wasted. When I clearly state what I mean and how committed I am to the idea or thought, others are better able to act quickly, decisively, and correctly. By clearly disclosing our objectives and intentions so others fully understand our Intent and Intensity, it makes it easier for us to achieve Right First Time interactions.

This enables everyone to calibrate how much to invest in a discussion, when to contribute ideas, and when to move to action. This makes life and work much easier for all of us!

The key to opening the door to understanding is to create clarity about our Intent and Intensity.

I am midway to completion of a high-priority project when George, a senior leader, walks by and asks how things are going.

When I tell him what I am working on, he smiles, leans closer, and says, "That is interesting! Have you thought about this?" He mentions an idea my team had already explored but decided would be more expensive and time-consuming than the approach we adopted.

Before I can find a diplomatic way to reply, George says, "You know, our Asian office is working on a similar program. You might want to check out what they are doing."

Then he looks at his watch, shakes his head, and says, "Late for a meeting. Got to go. Nice talking with you." And he is gone.

So now what do I do?

Do I call my team together and tell them we need to go back and take the slower, more expensive approach?

Did his comments constitute a career-dependent Go Do?

At XYZ Company, People Count

Several groups of senior leaders were visiting one of their company's production sites. As part of making conversation with one of the local managers, one of the visiting leaders offhandedly remarked, "I wonder how many valves there are at this site?"

That night, a team stayed up all night to count all the valves.

It certainly was not the leader's intent to have people engage in this behavior; the question was just a passing comment. But without explicit clarity about *Intent and Intensity* (i.e., the leader's intent regarding having someone provide a response to the thought), an idle question turned into an action that wasted a lot of people's time and energy.

All Thoughts, Suggestions, and Ideas Are Not Created Equal

In our work with organizations around the world, we have noticed a common problem among CEOs, middle managers, individual contributors, and front-line team members: None of them is a mind reader or telepath. None of them can tell exactly how their words and ideas are being interpreted by others. None of them can be certain whether or how their meanings and intentions have been heard or understood without conversation.

Sometimes a leader or a team member will make a statement to stimulate debate and discussion. It might be a spur-of-the-moment idea, or it could be something the person has been chewing on for a while and wants to share with others and to hear what they think.

Sometimes a leader will share something with such intensity and passion that it might sound like a directive, when in reality, the leader was just excited about the idea and did not intend anyone to act on it automatically or without a great deal more discussion or direction.

Sometimes people will make a calm, quiet statement that is reflective of something they feel strongly about, and which is intended as a clear directive with a call for action and execution that is not open for discussion.

Without extrasensory abilities or a commitment to regular use of a common language to clarify the *Intent and Intensity* of statements like these, misinterpretations and missteps are *inevitable*.

Without *Understanding*, Waste Is *Inevitable*

Without a means for clarifying the true intent and intensity of our communications, we run the risk of creating distractions, diluting our messages, and even sabotaging our intended outcomes. If people don't understand whether our comments are up-to-you suggestions or must-do directions for actions they need to take, a lot of time and energy is wasted.

The door to understanding won't open . . .

- if you don't know my expectations and I don't know yours.

- if I don't know how strongly committed you are to the idea you just shared.

- if I don't know whether a remark was intended as something just to think about, something to respond to and build upon, or something that is nonnegotiable and requiring immediate and specific action.

THE COMMON PROBLEM OF "DRIVE-BY" COMMUNICATIONS

Our focus on clarifying people's intentions and their levels of commitment to their intentions grew out of hearing people talking about how their leaders would constantly change the scope of their projects with "drive-by" comments and suggestions.

Our solution: a means to quickly, simply, and surely communicate and understand the nature and priority of a statement. That was the origin of

NOTIONS

STAKES

BOULDERS

and

TOMBSTONES

NOTIONS are statements that don't require any action from others.

A *Notion* is an in-the-shower idea or a hallway thought, offered as an invitation for further discussion. It is just a *Notion*—something that has not been given much thought and that does not have a lot of vested interest attached to it.

When a leader makes a casual statement such as "Maybe we should look into cloud computing for the office," or "Wouldn't it be great if we could all rotate jobs one day each month," it could easily become an action item unless prefaced by the phrase, "Here's a *Notion*" or "This is just a *Notion*."

Without that additional clarification, the team could easily interpret the comments as, "We better look into cloud computing," or "We should establish a job-rotation schedule." And that could mean a great deal of unexpected, unintended, and wasted effort.

A *Notion* is an invitation to have a discussion. By positioning a statement as a *Notion*, we open the door to exploring the idea and seeing where it will take the group. The pathway and outcome are not predetermined but rather open for joint discovery.

STAKES express a firmer position on an idea or issue.

Like the stakes we put into the ground to stabilize a tent, *Stakes* establish a place for the potential solution or discussion to start—but that place is intended to be moveable.

Imagine someone in a planning meeting saying, "We need to open a new distribution center in the Southwest. We should build it in Albuquerque." That could be interpreted as a demand to start building in Albuquerque and reorganizing, depending on how people hear implications of the statement.

But a different discussion follows if that person says, "We need to do something about distribution in the Southwest. My *Stake* is we build a new distribution center in Albuquerque."

That opens the door to a discussion that might include a new distribution center in Albuquerque as a solution to the distribution issues but also might turn to other possibilities such as leasing a larger fleet of trucks, expanding distribution centers in Colorado and Texas, or pulling out of the Southwest market.

Saying, "Here is my *Stake* on this issue . . ." opens the door to understanding by . . .

- clarifying your *current* position on the idea or issue based on the current facts and reasoning available to you.

- inviting others to supply additional sets of facts and alternative lines of reasoning with a goal of arriving at the optimum assessment of the issue and the best decision possible.

Although you have set a *Stake*, you are inviting others to join you in determining the best possible location for that *Stake*.

When you put your *Stake* in the ground and demonstrate that you are willing, eager, and able to move it, you are saying that no one of us is smarter than all of us, and that others may have insights and information that might reveal a better position for that *Stake*.

There is an implied belief that by stimulating others to respond to your *Stake*, it will enhance the idea: the wisdom of all of us involved will emerge, and the idea will be better than when it started.

BOULDERS offer little wiggle room.

Unlike a *Stake,* a *Boulder* is an item requiring action—a high priority. Someone who makes a *Boulder* statement has a strong investment in seeing the idea addressed in the way she or he has framed it. While a *Boulder* is not an invitation to discussion, requests for clarification and suggestions for implementation strategies might be accepted and even appreciated.

When you say, "This is a *Boulder* for me . . ." it implies that a considerable amount of energy and very persuasive information will be required by others to change your position and the direction of your desired decision and action. *Boulders* can be moved, but not easily!

Warning: *Boulder* statements should not be made with great frequency since that suggests there is little openness to being influenced or to change the decision, and the impact may be that team members stop bringing their thinking or opinions to the table.

TOMBSTONES

mean "this issue is not negotiable."

A *Tombstone* also means "You can have my badge over this one," "Forget about any discussion," or "Over my dead body!" When you label a statement a *Tombstone*, it indicates your total commitment to the idea or issue—so much so that you may be willing to leave your job if the action is not carried out or if you are asked to do something you are absolutely not willing to do. Often, *Tombstones* are about core values or beliefs, and to take or not take the action would violate your integrity and sense of who you are. Sometimes a *Tombstone* is an edict from above. The message is "just do it" and there is no sense in people spending time in discussion. In general, *Tombstone* statements should be made only in critical situations, when personal or organizational integrity is at issue.

Guide to Notions, Stakes,

Initiator has a:	Intent
	Discussion Possible
	Discussion Initiation
	Discussion Critical
	Discussion, if any, under duress

Boulders, & Tombstones

Intensity of Commitment	Desired Response
• Low investment • Individual is willing to let go of the idea • Testing if idea makes sense to others and/or hoping others will build upon the idea	Discuss if interested/to be explored, action optional
• States a position • Some investment • Wants to hear others' thoughts to get their perspectives/street corners and additions	Discuss, to be considered or explored in depth, acted upon if parties agree after discussion
• Strong investment • Firmly entrenched • Want it to happen This level of acting on an idea or making a decision should not be used frequently.	Action expected, substantive objections somewhat OK
• Total investment, worth quitting over This level of acting on an idea or making a decision should not be used frequently.	Act now, or else

Abdul's Badge

When Ingrid was on leave, her company went through a reorganization process in which her position was identified for elimination. The leader in charge of the reorganization instructed Abdul, Ingrid's manager, to notify her that her job was being eliminated.

Abdul refused, saying it was a *Tombstone* for him. It violated his personal code of ethics to eliminate her job while she was out on leave when there had been a commitment that she would have a job when she returned. He also felt it was a betrayal of the company's values.

The leader appreciated Abdul's candor and his desire to defend the values of the company. He worked with Abdul to reassign Ingrid temporarily to a new but comparable position and then support her in her transition.

"This Is Just a *Notion* . . ."

One of the reasons some people in organizations turn into yes-women or yes-men is their inability to distinguish the *Intent and Intensity* of team leaders' statements.

They may be afraid to offer their different perspectives because they fear the sender's statement is really a *Boulder* or *Tombstone*—a statement that cannot be easily discussed or influenced—when, in fact, it might just be a *Stake* or even a *Notion* expressed with passion.

That is why when you preface an in-the-shower idea or a hallway thought with a clear statement of *Intent and Intensity*, it doesn't just prevent misunderstandings; it can also stimulate greater participation in discussions. Conversely, if you intend a statement to be a *Boulder* or *Tombstone,* but you are not explicit about your *Intent and Intensity* (i.e., you did not use the words *Boulder* or *Tombstone*), there can be unwanted pushback and a lack of responsiveness, which can result in key deadlines and opportunities being missed.

Whether you are a leader or a team member, if you fail to share your opinion or expertise, your knowledge will be missing from the conversation. This results in wasted effort, false starts, and extra time spent redoing tasks, all of which suboptimize the talents of *every* team member, including the team leader.

Too much of anything can cause problems, and one of the benefits of defining *Intent and Intensity* in terms of *Notions, Stakes, Boulders,* and *Tombstones* is that we can begin to notice how frequently we tend to use each of them. While expressing *Notions* can be a great tool for opening the door to creativity and innovation, too many *Notions* can lead to a lack of decisive action. On the other hand, too many *Tombstones* result in the death of new thinking and energy for innovation.

Opening the Door to Understanding Yourself

Before I can make my Intent and Intensity clear to others, I must first be clear about them to myself. Asking "What are my intentions in making this statement?" often yields valuable insights. I may realize I have not considered what my intentions are or how strongly I feel about a given idea or perspective.

Making a habit out of clarifying *Intent and Intensity* helps you take greater ownership of your ideas and also reduces confusion.

So What's Stopping You from Wanting to *State Your Intent and Intensity?*

“I want to see what kind of reaction I get before I commit. If the boss doesn't like my idea, I don't want to be tied to it.”

“Isn't it obvious what I mean? If they are not sure what I mean, they should ask me. I can't help it if they are afraid to ask.”

“I feel awkward. I am not used to stating my intentions. We don't talk that way around here.”

- Taking responsibility for our own ideas and statements can require us to *Lean into Discomfort*. If you are afraid your boss will criticize your idea—or you for having raised it—it might help to let the boss know that in order to share it you will need to *Lean into Discomfort*. Then, if she is willing to *Listen as an Ally*, she will understand and appreciate your *Notions* or *Stakes*.

- It is common not to take the extra time to clarify meanings, intentions, and priorities that you believe ought to be obvious. And often it is hard to ask others what they really mean. But the extra time and effort eliminates waste and missteps in the long run.

- When we disclose our intentions, we do more than simply reduce the possibility of misunderstanding and make the act of listening easier. We also offer an invitation to others to reciprocate and disclose their intentions, which promotes cooperation, collaboration, and a greater sense of safety for us all. It might be awkward at first, but that's another reason why the first key, *Lean into Discomfort*, is so important.

A Boulder with Some Stakes

A team was working on its strategic plan at an off-site meeting. Wei Choong, the team leader, started the meeting by saying, "Here's my *Boulder*: We are going to increase our production by 30% within the next 18 months. If you agree or disagree, I need to hear that now."

After a very brief discussion, everyone agreed that they would fully support the direction and time frame. They were aware that additional discussion would only waste valuable time since Wei Choong's mind was firmly made up!

With the goals defined, it was time to discuss their implementation plans. Wei Choong had spent quite some time thinking about ways the team might approach achieving the production goal, but she believed the team could offer valuable contributions to the plan. In opening that phase of the discussion, she said, "Here are my *Stakes*—which I am willing to move—and here are some of my *Notions* . . ."

The team had a very engaged discussion, at the end of which they had agreement and ownership on their path forward. With clarity about the leader's and each other's *Intent and Intensity*, they opened the door to understanding, which yielded alignment among team members and a clear path forward.

Checklist for Stating Intent and Intensity

☑ Make *Notions, Stakes, Boulders*, and *Tombstones* common language for how the team will engage.

☑ Clarify that your passion on a topic does not mean you are closed to hearing other perspectives. Let people know that your *Stakes* and *Notions*, even when stated passionately, are still just *Stakes* and *Notions*.

☑ Actively seek feedback from team members on how often you use the range of *Intent* and *Intensity*. (Too many *Notions* and *Stakes* can be distracting. Too many *Boulders* or *Tombstones* can be dispiriting.)

☑ *Lean into Discomfort, Listen as an Ally*, and hear others' *Street Corners* to fully engage the team for greater understanding.

Opening the Door to

Key #4: Share Your Street Corner

Share Your Street Corner

- **SHARE YOUR PERSPECTIVE:** recognize you have a piece of the puzzle.

- **ACCEPT OTHERS' PERSPECTIVES:** as true for them.

- **BE CURIOUS:** hear another perspective as different, not wrong.

Most intersections have four street corners. Some have even more. The challenge is to hear from all the Street Corners! Don't assume your view is the only view, the best view, or even the correct view.

I am standing at a busy intersection, waiting to cross the street, when I hear a screech of brakes. I look up just in time to see a large black SUV plow into the rear passenger door of a red sedan, which spins around and smacks into the front left quarter panel of a parked minivan.

Fortunately, no one appears to be injured. From my vantage point on my street corner, I can see the drivers of the vehicles involved in the accident getting out of their cars, each pointing a finger of blame at the other.

Uh oh, I think. They are going to have trouble sorting this out. It looked like the SUV may have been to blame, but the red sedan may have run a traffic light. I was an eyewitness, but I really can't say who was at fault.

Without the full range of perspectives, we cannot be sure we have the complete picture.

What Is the View from *Your Street Corner?*

So how do the police sort things out? They start by asking themselves, "What do we need to know to figure out what happened?"

As they question the people involved in the accident and the witnesses at the scene, they do not assume that any one person can give them the full picture. Ideally, they want to get reports from witnesses on all four corners of the intersection—preferably, several from each corner, from the people crossing the street, and the people who were involved in the accident—so they get the fullest picture of what took place.

Once they gather as many viewpoints and details as possible, they come together, share what they learned, and put all the data together until a fully dimensional, 360-degree, time-sequenced picture of the incident emerges so they can solve the puzzle.

If they discover that none of them has spoken to any witnesses from the southwest corner, they may decide to go back to the scene to see if they can find more witnesses.

The reason? Even if the witnesses from the other corners have provided what seems to be a complete accounting of the accident, there would be a gap from the southwest perspective. And while it is possible that southwest-corner witnesses may have nothing new to add, there is also the very real possibility that those witnesses may have seen something that could not have been seen from any other angle.

Without accounting for all the *Street Corners*, they may fail to get the breakthrough information that solves the puzzle.

We all need to be willing to share our *Street Corners*

There are a lot of things happening in our team. But I can't and don't know everything. That is why you need to Share Your Street Corner constantly—responsively and proactively—and I need to share mine. I need to ask you what you are seeing from Your Street Corner, and I need to be ready to Listen as an Ally when you share that information.

And if I think it could help you, I need to tell you about what I see from my Street Corner, even if you don't ask.

Because so many unknowns and unknowables exist in today's organizations, it is essential to get as many views as possible to solve complex challenges and problems. In this highly competitive marketplace, businesses can no longer afford to make many mistakes. When time, energy, and money are wasted because all the right players weren't involved in the first place, or decisions need to be reconsidered because critical information did not get incorporated during the problem-solving process, the whole organization suffers.

We need to expand our comfort zones around who is involved, when they are involved in the process, and how their perspectives are heard.

Our First To-Do

If we want to make sure we are getting the complete picture, if we want to avoid false starts and mistakes, and if we want *Right First Time* decisions, actions, and interactions, the first thing to do in order to understand the situation is to make sure we hear from all *Street Corners*. We need to assume there is a bigger picture, and the challenge is to get input from *all*. That is what is required to open the door to *breakthroughs*.

"What gets us into trouble is not what we don't know. It is what we know for sure that just ain't so."
—Mark Twain

The Key That Opens the Door to Breakthroughs

If I am willing to Lean into *the* Discomfort *of reaching out to you . . .*

If I am willing to Listen as an Ally *so I can hear and appreciate the different perspectives you have to offer . . .*

And if I am willing to State *my* Intent and Intensity *so you and others can understand where I am coming from . . .*

. . . then *we have the possibility to gain from others'* Street Corners *and create something new together: a* breakthrough!

Even if my view is incomplete, I can't assume that I can't contribute. I have a piece of the puzzle that will help the group to arrive at a more complete picture of the situation.

Wrong OR Different?

I am in a meeting, and Jane expresses a different perspective from mine. It seems like she is just playing devil's advocate again. Instead of being curious and inquiring about her position, I label her and her perspective—her Street Corner—as wrong.

She just doesn't understand the situation, I think. We are not aligned. And I see the difference as a conflict.

Seeing Value in Differences of Opinion

When we hear someone voicing a point of view differing from our own—bringing another *Street Corner*—we may tell that person, either with our words or through facial expressions, to be quiet. Or we may label someone who raises conflicting issues or highlights inconvenient information as not a team player. But this is a lot like shooting the messenger.

It is easy to see a different perspective or *Street Corner* as wrong and to label a potential contribution as a conflict. But by doing so, we miss the opportunity to see another view that can add value, eliminate missteps, or bring our discussion to a new level of thinking.

Sometimes what sounds like disagreement is really a different Street Corner.

Reaching Out to New *Street Corners*

The idea of seeking out a *Street Corner* other than our own—or other than the one held widely by a team or by the team leader—is sometimes framed as just looking for trouble. Often, differences of opinion are considered disruptive. Many times organizations are so entrenched in their hierarchy that they don't consider reaching out to other layers of the organization—areas where people may have another *Street Corner* or data that is crucial to the problem or decision at hand.

A lot of people, and a lot of teams, put a high value on agreement. They feel it is important for everyone to act and think uniformly. But uniformity can discourage new voices and ideas and hinder breakthroughs.

By insisting that everyone agrees, thinks the same way, and acts the same way, we might miss the 360-degree vision we need. We fall into groupthink and sameness.

As in a chemical reaction, the stimulus for higher achievement and innovation comes when the catalyst is added—bringing in new or different *Street Corners.*

I Need to Hear *Your Street Corner*

The work-teams at a large manufacturing site were reorganizing their processes in an effort to improve quality and productivity. The plant's future depended on these efforts; *everyone's* job was at stake.

People in frontline and operator-level positions were not accustomed to being asked to offer their opinions to their supervisors or managers. But they had all been working on changing the organizational interactions using the 4 Keys.

In one department's work process meeting, the team leader asked the frontline team members to provide input saying, "I need to hear your *Street Corners* to improve these processes."

Because of their work with the 4 Keys, everyone knew this statement meant: "Your point of view is important to our information-gathering and decision-making process. I need your honest, unvarnished view of the situation. Please don't just tell me what you think I want to hear!"

As a result, team members spoke up and the group was able to implement a series of process changes that improved productivity significantly. It was indeed a breakthrough for the department and the plant. Part of that productivity gain was attributed to the entire team's sense of ownership because they were willing to *Lean into Discomfort*, *Listen as Allies*, *State Intent and Intensity*, and *Share* their *Street Corners*.

So What's Stopping You from Wanting to *Share Your Street Corner?*

> ❝My Street Corner isn't very important. I am new here. I don't have the experience of the other people.❞

> ❝Asking for other opinions just wastes my time. Let us just agree to disagree and get on with it. We have deadlines to meet!❞

> ❝Too many perspectives just lead to conflict. I can't afford endless argument and debate. It takes too much time.❞

When you Share Your Street Corner, it isn't just making sure all perspectives are heard. You also need to make sure you are open to joining Street Corners different from your own.

- New people on the team may be reluctant to share their *Street Corners* because they feel unsure of their positions, feel they haven't proven themselves yet, or fear not being accepted by their colleagues. Yet they bring fresh eyes to a lot of situations. New people may see things that other members of the team can't see because, to them, everything looks normal, and it is just the way they *do* things.

- When we are working in firefighting mode, as so many of us are so much of the time, we may feel we are too busy to want to hear others' opinions. But often the firefighting mode is the result of having missed some critical information the last time a similar problem was addressed. In order to avoid revisiting issues or problems, we often need the information that comes from different *Street Corners*. In the long run, the fastest route includes hearing the differing opinions to arrive at the best solution.

- The biggest reason many people don't share their *Street Corners* is that they want to be seen as team players and want to avoid conflict. Colleagues may fear that offering a different *Street Corner* will be viewed as creating conflict and may therefore play it safe by just agreeing or not saying anything. But being curious about a different *Street Corner*— rather than seeing it as wrong—can turn what looked like conflict into a better outcome for all.

Another *Street Corner*

One of the internal leaders of an organizational change process invited a group of people she had been working with from other business units to a meeting of her internal team of Change Leaders.

She wanted the people from the other business units to observe a meeting in which the 4 Keys were part of the new normal.

The visitors were invited to share their ideas and provided valuable insights to the team's work. The team of Change Leaders said the outside group brought "another *Street Corner*" that helped the team's work be even better. And the visitors said they felt included and excited by the model they had seen for conducting a meeting.

The creative friction that happens when multiple ideas are rubbed together is a source of innovation and breakthroughs.

It's Not Faster if It's Not Right

The mistakes, snafus, and failures that result from acting with insufficient information have proven many times over that *Right First Time* processes are far more efficient, productive, and profitable than fast-but-not-right processes.

To *Lean into Discomfort, Listen as an Ally, State Intent and Intensity,* and reach out to make sure all *Street Corners* are shared may seem like a time-consuming process that can be skipped when time is tight, but when all 4 Keys are part of the organization's everyday interactions, *speed happens!*

Just because you are fast doesn't mean you have the best or only solution. Speed is important but not if you have to redo the work.

What Extra Time?

A group's revised meeting structure relied heavily on 360-degree feedback, making problems visible, and creating a safe environment to speak up. The meeting's convener had been diligent about asking for input from meeting participants to ensure that they were hearing from all *Street Corners*.

Though people had initially worried that hearing all the "extra" viewpoints would cost extra time, the group found it completed all of its agenda items within the time-frame allotted, while still ensuring time for idea generation and input.

Meeting attendees noted that the increased input was actually helping them to resolve issues faster as people focused on sharing their learning and experiences. Other groups were beginning to ask about this team's successes. The team's emphasis on working for the common good, getting the right people to do the right work at the right time, and making sure all *Street Corners* are heard made them true believers in the change.

To *Share Your Street Corner*, You Must . . .

- accept another person's experience, perspective, or position as true for them.

- be curious about why someone else sees something differently from the way you do.

- join and learn from other people's *Street Corners* rather than judge what they say as wrong.

- build on what someone else says to create something new and exciting for both of you.

Ask Who Else Needs to Be in the Room

One of the keys to success for any organization is having the *right people* doing the *right work* at the *right time*.

It seems easier and more comfortable to invite people from the same Street Corner *as mine to the meeting, but I am learning to be more intentional about making sure all potentially relevant viewpoints are included—even those that differ from my own. It increases my team's chances for producing* Right First Time *results and finding breakthrough solutions that none of us individually could imagine.*

*Are we the right people?
Who else needs to be here?
Asking the right questions
helps us get all the
different Street Corners!*

If you want to include all *Street Corners* . . .

- identify people, functions, and groups who will be impacted by decisions, and make sure to include the right people from those groups.

- Keep people in the loop. If one or two individuals are unable to attend, identify a buddy for each to make sure pertinent information from the meeting gets to them in a timely manner.

- ask the question "Are all the right people in the room?" It encourages everyone to think about who else might have valuable input that could help to solve problems and make decisions.

- postpone the meeting if some of the key players are not available. This eliminates waste by having the right people doing the right work at the right time. It also saves time by not having to revisit a decision because valuable input was missing.

Here's *My Street Corner*

The senior leader had been instrumental in improving the communication processes in her organization and was very aware of the need to *State Intent and Intensity* by labeling her ideas as *Notions* and *Stakes*.

She also wanted to be able to provide her team members with the benefit of her *Street Corner*, not only as a leader but as a person with unique background experiences on various situations without requiring those perspectives to be regarded as the only way of viewing the matter. To accomplish this, she labeled those ideas as *Sharing her Street Corner,* and she solicited honest opinions and feedback from her team by saying "I need to hear *Your Street Corner* on this."

Because of the leader's focus on clear, open, and honest discussion, the team functions at a very high level. Decisions are made quickly and effectively, with rapid and enthusiastic buy-in from the right people in the organization. The quality of these interactions enabled the team to open the door to breakthroughs because they had access to a multitude of *Street Corners* and therefore address challenges that no one person on the team could resolve.

Checklist for Inviting Others to Share Street Corners

☑ Invite others to *Share Street Corners,* thus opening the door for them to feel safe contributing.

☑ Treat others as experts on their own experience.

☑ Be open and curious to learn why and how others have reached the conclusions and ideas they present, particularly when they are different from yours.

☑ Find ways to build on what another person shared, and see if together you can find a new solution that neither of you individually could have imagined.

Last Words

OUR HOPES AND DREAMS

When we started writing this book, we initially were going to write about the *12 Inclusive Behaviors*—behaviors we have been sharing with our clients for many years because they have had a profound, positive impact on work cultures in which *Inclusion* is the foundation for *how* people work.

Then one day we were in a client meeting in which someone said, "We *love* the *12 Inclusive Behaviors*, but *these* 4 are the keys that change *everything*!"

Organizations face many challenges. And many people inside of them feel that their contributions don't matter. They feel powerless to make a difference or to have more positive interactions.

It may be easy to feel at times that our organizations and society are on the wrong path. Some are afraid that this current state of feeling powerless and fearful is what life in organizations is and will always be.

We have written this book because we are optimistic about where some organizations are going and what all organizations *can be*. Yes, we see all that is going on today and how hard it is for many people at all levels in organizations. And we feel sad that many cannot see or don't experience significant positive change today or in the foreseeable future.

But at the same time, we have seen organizations that *can* and *want to* be different. We have worked with organizations that have transformed themselves from being workplaces where people don't count and individuals and teams feel powerless into ones in which people find their voices, feel valued, and together achieve wonderful things—*breakthroughs*.

It is always helpful for us to remember our favorite quote from our favorite futurist, Mary O'Hara Devereaux: "The future is here, but not evenly distributed."

We have seen pockets of greatness in some of our client systems—unevenly distributed, for sure—but we know that greatness can spread. We thank our clients for that glimpse into making what *can be* a reality, and we thank the people of our consulting firm for helping nurture those pockets of success.

Some of what we see:

- There are people in organizations all over the world who have committed to live life differently—to improve their relationships by changing their interactions at work (and at home).

- Many people are working more hours and sacrificing more and more for work, and in doing so, many are becoming increasingly aware that they want more out of their interactions at work. They don't want to settle for underperforming, having to do rework, and feeling as if they don't matter—most people want to make a difference, want to have an impact.

- People are ready for a breakthrough!

We can't promise that this book is the breakthrough everyone needs. We *do* know it has been a breakthrough for *us* and many others. What we have shared in this book has enabled many people to have not only professional breakthroughs, but also personal ones as they apply the 4 Keys to create better, healthier interactions in all aspects of their lives.

It starts with realizing that if you want to have greater teamwork and collaboration (and greater speed in achieving effective teamwork and collaboration) that a *joining* mindset is critical. When you really see others as colleagues and allies, a new "we" sets the foundation to open doors and achieve things that no individual alone can achieve.

But the awareness of the need to join or even the desire to join with others is insufficient to open the doors to real teamwork. Without the willingness and ability to *Lean into Discomfort, Listen as an Ally, State Intent and Intensity*, and *Share Your Street Corner*, improvement for many organizations will not happen fast enough, and significant breakthroughs will not occur.

Collaboration, higher performance, and teamwork are not going to be achieved by wishing or wanting or waiting. *They require action!* They need a common language to reinforce and spread that understanding. They need a common set of behaviors. They need the 4 Keys That Change *Everything*.

And once you start using these Keys, you and your interactions will *never* be the same again.

Start Today

You can start putting these 4 Keys to work for you and your organization today. We hope that you do. As individuals, partners, teams, and organizations around the globe, none of us can afford to wait. The Keys are here for you to use.

The 4 Keys work even if you are the only one using them, because they give you the means to change the nature and quality of your interactions with others.

You can use them with your team members. You can use them with colleagues throughout the organization. You can use them with family members and friends, people in your community, people you see every day.

The more you use them, the better they will work for you because they will feel more natural.

The 4 Keys are simple, and if you adopt them as your standard way of interacting, you will change the quality of your relationships with other people. Your interactions will be enhanced, as will your life. The people you work with will start to treat you differently. They will join you. They will speak with you more openly and honestly, sharing their intentions, and partnering with you in new and exciting ways. Things will *feel* different, and you will experience life differently.

Doors will open

Why wait? What lie ahead are trust, understanding, collaboration, and breakthroughs for you and your team. And when the doors open, inside you will find the rewards of teamwork and collaboration, and *Everything* will change.

Acknowledgments

A book on teamwork and collaboration would not be possible without the many people who joined with us and gave so generously of their time and thinking to make *Opening Doors* possible.

First and foremost, thank you, Roger Gans, for your wit and dedication to helping our work shine. You "get" us and have helped us find the voice to make this book possible. Thanks for being a great partner.

Tara Whittle, we have sincere appreciation for you, for your thorough review of the book, for your creativity in working with Brian Murray to get the front and back covers just right, and for always bringing another *Street Corner* that enhances our work.

Thank you, Victoria Gammerman, for initially shepherding the book through its creation, and to Julie Bush, for bringing this to fruition. You both have played valuable roles in helping us realize this important project.

Opening Doors would not be the book it is without our fabulous editor, Steve Piersanti. Thank you, Steve, for continuing to demonstrate your faith in us, for leaning in to challenge us as allies in order to make the book and its concepts even more alive and useful for others, and for pushing us to be our best. We appreciate the trust, collaboration, and partnership we have with you. You are indeed a publisher like no other.

Jeevan Sivasubramaniam, we thank you and appreciate the many hats you wear and the many roles you have played in making *Opening Doors* a reality. First, in your day job as managing editor, and second, for the life you breathed into the book through your illustrations.

We thank the Berrett-Koehler staff and their partners—Dave Peattie and Tanya Grove of BookMatters, Catherine Lengronne, Charlotte Ashlock, Courtney Schonfeld, David Marshall, Katie Sheehan, Kristin Frantz, Maria Jesus Aguil, Marina Cook, Mike Crowley, Rick Wilson, and Zoe Mackey—for continuing to bring a level of excellence to ensure that this book and other BK books are a cut above the rest. A big thank you to Dianne Platner for her artistic vision and partnership when it was really needed.

Our reviewers and friends—Kenneth Fracaro, Leigh Wilkinson, Libba Pinchot, Regina Sacha-Ujczo, and Sandy Chase—all provided *Street Corners* that challenged our thinking. Catherine Volk, Corey Jamison, Peter Norlin, and David Levine—we give you much appreciation for your thoughtful comments and reviews.

Many of the ideas in *Opening Doors* were continually shaped by our clients. Many thanks and much appreciation to Steve Fritze, retired CFO of Ecolab, for expanding our thinking and coining the term

"Challenging as an Ally" and to Anthony Abbattista, Principal at Deloitte Consulting and formerly SVP of Technology Solutions at Allstate, for his contributions to our thinking about Boulders and Tombstones. We appreciate and have been influenced by Mary O'Hara Devereaux's book, *Navigating the Badlands: Thriving in the Decade of Radical Transformation* (2004, Jossey Bass) and highly recommend it to others who are thinking about change today.

We send *big* thank yous to the Core Inclusion and and Change Partners from around the world; as well as to Bridget O'Brien, Diane Krell, Gae Angoh, Hugh MacDonald, Julie Arnell, Martin Inskip, Nadine Mackey, Stan Howell, Walter Slade, and Willie Deese for showing us the 4 Keys in action and how they are making a difference for their organizations. We thank our partners as well—KengChoo and Eunice Chan from Caliper in Singapore, and Sushma Sharma in India. And we thank our friends at Community 2022 for their insights in strengthening the notions of Judging and Joining.

A big thank you goes out to all the members of The Kaleel Jamison Consulting Group for their support of us every day and for their work on the book—the consultants for sharing their thinking and our great Troy Hub team for making this book happen!

And to the people who every day were willing to lean in and trust us, to try something new, and to learn with us—you each had a piece of this puzzle and helped to create the whole.

It does take a village to create a book. Thanks to our village around the globe for opening these doors with us.

About the Authors

Judith H. Katz and
Frederick A. Miller

For more than 30 years, individually and together, Judith Katz and Fred Miller have been working to transform organizations and the ways people interact with one another within them.

They started their business partnership in 1985, Judith coming from faculty positions at the Universities of Oklahoma and San Diego State, and Fred from management positions at Connecticut General Life Insurance Company. It was a major turning point in both their lives.

As Executive Vice President and CEO (respectively)

for The Kaleel Jamison Consulting Group, Inc.—one of *Consulting* magazine's Seven Small Jewels in 2010—they have partnered with Fortune 100 and other companies to elevate the quality of interactions, leverage people's differences, and transform workplaces into growth-and-learning environments in which people's talents are unleashed, results are accelerated, and productivity soars. Their partnership is proof that teamwork and collaboration does create breakthroughs.

Through their thought leadership and practical applications to changing workplaces, they have brought their unique perspective, passion, and energy to make a difference in the lives of organizations and individuals that few can match.

In addition to many other writings, together they have co-authored three books:

- *The Inclusion Breakthrough: Unleashing the Real Power of Diversity* (2002)

- *Be BIG: Step Up, Step Out, Be Bold* (2008)

- *Opening Doors to Teamwork and Collaboration: 4 Keys That Change Everything* (2013)

Judith and Fred have each been honored with several of their fields' most distinguished awards. In 2007, *Profiles in Diversity Journal* named them two of 40 Pioneers of Diversity, and in 2012, they were each honored as Legends of Diversity by the International

Society of Diversity and Inclusion Professionals. Among other awards they have received is Fred's Lifetime Achievement Award, presented by the Organization Development Network (ODN) and Judith's Outstanding Achievement in Global Work Award, also from the ODN.

Their consulting practice, workshops, and conference presentations have impacted clients and groups in the United States, Singapore, India, China, Thailand, the United Kingdom, Australia, the Netherlands, and Mexico.

Judith loves fishing and traveling with David, her husband.

Fred is a workaholic who loves being at home with his marriage partner, Pauline.

Judith's extraversion and Fred's introversion often have them seeing the world from different *Street Corners* that have led to many intense conversations, personal and professional revelations—and a lot of laughter and creativity.

They are already working on their next breakthrough.

Also by Judith H. Katz and Frederick A. Miller

Be BIG

Step Up, Step Out, Be Bold

Too many people have decided that the safest way to get through life is to be small. But organizations need people to step up and Be BIG. People must bring more of themselves to the workplace in order to contribute more and have a bigger impact. Winner of the 2009 National Indie Excellence Award for Regional Nonfiction and the 2009 Next Generation Indie Book Award in the Motivational category, *Be BIG* challenges all of us to show up more fully to work—as individuals and in our interactions with others—as we find ways to Be BIG together.

"Judith and Fred have written the ultimate guide to career development. A perfect book to create a dialogue with peers, direct reports or friends."

—Beverly Kaye, founder and CEO, Career Systems International, and coauthor of *Help Them Grow or Watch Them Go* and *Love 'Em or Lose 'Em*

Paperback, 96 pages, ISBN 978-1-57675-452-8
PDF ebook, ISBN 978-1-57675-784-0

BK® Berrett–Koehler Publishers, Inc.
San Francisco, *www.bkconnection.com*   800.929.2929

The Inclusion Breakthrough
Unleashing the Real Power of Diversity

The Inclusion Breakthrough proves that making diversity and inclusion a central part of organizational strategy, rather than a peripheral program, can help organizations achieve success and gain a competitive advantage. The authors show precisely how to implement a specific, tested, and proven methodology for systemic change that will unleash the nearly boundless creativity and productivity of any organization's greatest resource: its people. Based on real-world business practices, these practical strategies for systemic change will lead to a more powerful and passionate workforce and an improved bottom line.

"A must-read for organizations that want to move diversity work to a new level."

—Ken Blanchard, author of *Great Leaders Grow* and *The One Minute Manager*

Paperback, 240 pages, ISBN 978-1-57675-139-8
PDF ebook, ISBN 978-1-60509-427-4

Berrett–Koehler Publishers, Inc.
San Francisco, *www.bkconnection.com*

800.929.2929

Berrett–Koehler
Publishers

Berrett-Koehler is an independent publisher dedicated to an ambitious mission: *Creating a World That Works for All*.

We believe that to truly create a better world, action is needed at all levels—individual, organizational, and societal. At the individual level, our publications help people align their lives with their values and with their aspirations for a better world. At the organizational level, our publications promote progressive leadership and management practices, socially responsible approaches to business, and humane and effective organizations. At the societal level, our publications advance social and economic justice, shared prosperity, sustainability, and new solutions to national and global issues.

A major theme of our publications is "Opening Up New Space." Berrett-Koehler titles challenge conventional thinking, introduce new ideas, and foster positive change. Their common quest is changing the underlying beliefs, mindsets, institutions, and structures that keep generating the same cycles of problems, no matter who our leaders are or what improvement programs we adopt.

We strive to practice what we preach—to operate our publishing company in line with the ideas in our books. At the core of our approach is stewardship, which we define as a deep sense of responsibility to administer the company for the benefit of all of our "stakeholder" groups: authors, customers, employees, investors, service providers, and the communities and environment around us.

We are grateful to the thousands of readers, authors, and other friends of the company who consider themselves to be part of the "BK Community." We hope that you, too, will join us in our mission.

A BK Business Book

This book is part of our BK Business series. BK Business titles pioneer new and progressive leadership and management practices in all types of public, private, and nonprofit organizations. They promote socially responsible approaches to business, innovative organizational change methods, and more humane and effective organizations.

Berrett–Koehler
Publishers

A community dedicated to creating
a world that works for all

Visit Our Website: www.bkconnection.com

Read book excerpts, see author videos and Internet movies, read
our authors' blogs, join discussion groups, download book apps,
find out about the BK Affiliate Network, browse subject-area
libraries of books, get special discounts, and more!

Subscribe to Our Free E-Newsletter, the *BK Communiqué*

Be the first to hear about new publications, special discount
offers, exclusive articles, news about bestsellers, and more!
Get on the list for our free e-newsletter by going to **www
.bkconnection.com**.

Get Quantity Discounts

Berrett-Koehler books are available at quantity discounts for
orders of ten or more copies. Please call us toll-free at (800)
929-2929 or email us at **bkp.orders@aidcvt.com**.

Join the BK Community

BKcommunity.com is a virtual meeting place where people
from around the world can engage with kindred spirits to create
a world that works for all. **BKcommunity.com** members may
create their own profiles, blog, start and participate in forums
and discussion groups, post photos and videos, answer surveys,
announce and register for upcoming events, and chat with others
online in real time. Please join the conversation!

SUSTAINABLE FORESTRY INITIATIVE
Label applies to the text stock
Certified Sourcing
www.sfiprogram.org
SFI-00341

Certified

Corporation
bcorporation.net